Making Change Work

Practical Tools for Overcoming Human Resistance to Change

Brien Palmer

ASQ Quality Press
Milwaukee, Wisconsin

American Society for Quality, Quality Press, Milwaukee 53203

© 2004 by ASQ

All rights reserved. Published 2003

Printed in the United States of America

12 11 10 09 08 07 06   5 4 3

Library of Congress Cataloging-in-Publication Data

Palmer, Brien, 1952–
  Making change work : practical tools for overcoming human resistance
to change / Brien Palmer.
    p. cm.
  Includes bibliographical references and index.
  ISBN 0-87389-611-4 (pbk. : alk. paper)
  1. Organizational change. I. Title.

  HD58.8.P346 2003
  658.4'06—dc22   2003020728

ISBN 0-87389-611-4

Publisher: William A. Tony
Acquisitions Editor: Annemieke Hytinen
Project Editor: Paul O'Mara
Production Administrator: Barbara Mitrovic
Special Marketing Representative: David Luth

ASQ Mission: The American Society for Quality advances individual,
organizational, and community excellence worldwide through learning,
quality improvement, and knowledge exchange.

Attention Bookstores, Wholesalers, Schools, and Corporations: ASQ Quality
Press books, videotapes, audiotapes, and software are available at quantity
discounts with bulk purchases for business, educational, or instructional use.
For information, please contact ASQ Quality Press at 800-248-1946, or write to
ASQ Quality Press, P.O. Box 3005, Milwaukee, WI 53201-3005.

To place orders or to request a free copy of the ASQ Quality Press Publications
Catalog, including ASQ membership information, call 800-248-1946. Visit our
Web site at www.asq.org or http://qualitypress.asq.org.

∞ Printed on acid-free paper

Quality Press
600 N. Plankinton Avenue
Milwaukee, Wisconsin 53203
Call toll free 800-248-1946
Fax 414-272-1734
www.asq.org
http://qualitypress.asq.org
http://standardsgroup.asq.org
E-mail: authors@asq.org

ASQ
AMERICAN SOCIETY
FOR QUALITY™

Making Change Work

Practical Tools for Overcoming Human Resistance to Change

Also available from ASQ Quality Press:

The Executive Guide to Improvement and Change
G. Dennis Beecroft, Grace L. Duffy, John W. Moran

From Quality to Business Excellence: A Systems Approach to Management
Charles Cobb

The Change Agent's Guide to Radical Improvement
Ken Miller

The Change Agents' Handbook: A Survival Guide for Quality Improvement Champions
David W. Hutton

Strategic Navigation: A Systems Approach to Business Strategy
H. William Dettmer

Principles and Practices of Organizational Performance Excellence
Thomas J. Cartin

From Baldrige to the Bottom Line: A Road Map for Organizational Change and Improvement
David W. Hutton

Customer Centered Six Sigma: Linking Customers, Process Improvement, and Financial Results
Earl Naumann and Steven H. Hoisington

The Certified Quality Manager Handbook, Second Edition
Duke Okes and Russell T. Westcott, editors

To request a complimentary catalog of ASQ Quality Press publications, call (800) 248-1946, or visit our bookstore at http://www.asq.org.

Table of Contents

List of Figures and Tables

Preface

Change has a considerable psychological impact on the human mind. To the fearful it is threatening because it means that things may get worse. To the hopeful it is encouraging because things may get better. To the confident it is inspiring because the challenge exists to make things better.

—King Whitney Jr.

This book was written for people trying to improve their organizations, such as executives, managers, project sponsors, project leaders, team leaders, and team members. All improvement requires change, and all change causes a predictable *resistance* by those people who are affected by the change. Unfortunately, this tendency—the lack of acceptance of the change—often causes a project to fail, even if the desired change is perfectly logical and necessary.

This book will help change leaders, particularly technical managers, understand and deal with the human aspect of change. The ability to deal with the *human* elements can mean the difference between the success or failure of a project—or a career!

WHAT THIS BOOK PROVIDES

This book will help you in several ways. First, it provides tools to measure your organization's readiness to change. Do *not* attempt a change until you have demonstrated your organization's readiness. The price of a failed change is a widespread loss of credibility of the noble objective that you were trying to achieve. That price is too high.

It also provides an easily understood model for making sure that your change project will be accepted by the organization (see Figure 1). This

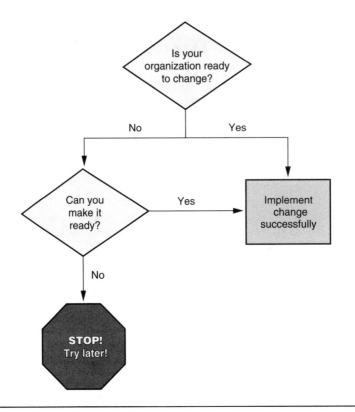

Figure 1 Making change work.

model is not academic—it provides a framework for hands-on actions designed to gain the organization's acceptance of the change you are trying to make. It also provides your team with a way to work together effectively on this project.

Finally, and perhaps most significantly, this book provides many practical tools to apply sequentially and logically at specific stages of your project. The tools are illustrated with actual examples from real companies. The layout of the model and the tools in the book mimics the structure of a well-designed project. This structure will appeal to technical and project-oriented people and provide practical structure to an area (human behavior) often viewed as *soft* or nebulous.

These tools and principles work best if they are shared openly with all members of your core team. They should comprise an integral part of the project plan. Encourage open and frank communication about *change management* issues throughout your project. If you have internal opposition, lack of management support, or other obstacles, name them. Use the tools to quantify them and take appropriate action. The use of candid communication and shared leadership will encourage personal growth and help develop a stronger team.

CHANGE HAPPENS

Some change will always happen but not necessarily the change you want. It is far better to plan for and manage change systematically, rather than simply react to events as they occur. This book will help you do just that. Best of luck to you and your team!

Introduction

Change comes in all sizes, from one person simply doing something slightly different to major programs involving thousands of people. This book applies best to any change that requires a *project:* a group of people with dedicated resources working towards a defined end. Examples of projects might include:

- Installing a new software system such as an inventory control system

- Developing a new administrative process such as a 360° performance evaluation

- Implementing an organizational change such as a restructuring

- Introducing new technology such as voice recognition software

- Moving to a new location or opening a new facility

- Creating a new product or service

WHY CHANGE FAILS

An incredibly high percentage of changes introduced in business organizations do not reach their full potential—that is, do not reach full implementation or do not produce the benefits envisioned by their sponsors.

Changes that fail usually do not fail because of *technical* reasons—something inherently flawed about the change itself. They usually fail because of *human* reasons—the promoters of the change did not attend to the healthy, real, and predictable reactions of normal people to disturbances in their routines (see Figure 2).

These failures create large losses of time, productivity, and morale. They also undercut the legitimate business objectives that the change was meant to engender. For example, one manufacturer attempted to replace

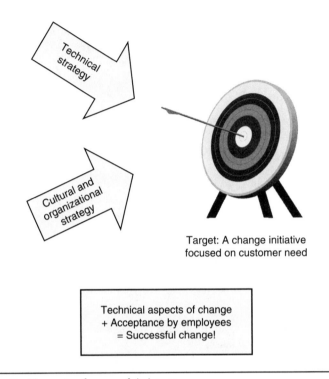

Target: A change initiative
focused on customer need

Technical aspects of change
+ Acceptance by employees
= Successful change!

Figure 2   Elements of successful change.

several disjointed software systems with one integrated enterprise resource planning (ERP) system. Because of poor project management, the user community was insufficiently involved in the planning stages, and the project failed dramatically. Opponents then said, "Told you, we just can't do an ERP in our business." In fact, having an ERP was a great idea. The project failed because of poor *change management* practices, and it took years for the organization to recover and install an ERP successfully.

This human tendency to want consistency—to resist change—is actually *healthy,* in the balance. Without consistency, life would fall out of control and into chaos. We would be unable to predict people's behaviors or establish our own routines and positive behavioral patterns. Thank goodness for the steadying force of our own behavioral inertia.

However, this same steadying force can work against us when we try to introduce a change. People tend not to want to deviate from behaviors that work for them.

Why do they not want to change when the need for change is so clear to you? It is precisely because the need for change is *not* clear to them. It is often said that people don't resist *change* so much as they resist *being changed*. So your job is clear: in a nutshell, you have to explain why the affected people should *want* to change. You have to convey the same understanding and enthusiasm that you and your team have. You have to cultivate readiness, not resistance.

This book provides specific tools and principles to accomplish this task. Using these tools will make change work.

Measure Your Organization's Readiness for Change

This chapter provides tools for you and your team to use in evaluating whether your organization is prepared for a change. It also helps highlight specific areas that need work before you start. The first tool helps determine if your organization is unable to absorb any more change. The second tool evaluates your readiness with respect to the change model introduced in the next chapter.

As with most of the tools throughout, these evaluations are best done as a team effort. You might invite your sponsor, unless you feel that his or her presence could hinder the open exchange of ideas. A sponsor can be defined as a manager with the authority to provide revenues, authorize people's involvement, and gain the organizational acceptance sufficient to implement the project.

CAN YOUR ORGANIZATION ABSORB ANY MORE CHANGE EFFORTS?

The ability of any organization to assimilate change is finite. No matter how worthy your project is, it will not succeed if your organization faces too many other changes. Picture a sponge filled to capacity—it will not pick up more water until some capacity opens up.

In general, you should not undertake any project unless it has a reasonable chance of success. In management consulting circles, for example, there is a general reluctance to accept an engagement that has a likelihood of failure. Many consultants consider it unethical to accept such a project.

First, determine if your organization has more than a 50 percent chance of having the capacity to make *this* change without becoming overwhelmed. To do so, list all of the major ongoing activities that will compete for manpower, money, and attention. Estimate the level of effort that each project will take (small, medium, or large). Then, estimate the level of effort required by this current project. (Be sure to consider all the activities recommended in this book.) Finally, consider the current load of the organization. Most organizations already run lean, so they have limited time to address any additional efforts.

Hold a dialogue with team members and use good judgment to estimate the chance of success for this project. If you are near 50 percent, you are risking too much. In all likelihood, your estimate is already too optimistic, since your team is probably emotionally invested in it. If you do not see a high chance for success—for example, 85 percent—you should defer the work until more favorable times. It is better to have a successful project at a future date than a stressful and unsuccessful one now.

In any case, the more change that the organization is undergoing, the more important the topics in this book become. Next, move beyond your organization's ability to absorb more change and examine its readiness for the project in question.

HOW PREPARED IS YOUR ORGANIZATION FOR *THIS* CHANGE?

Ask each team member to consider the current project and rate your readiness with respect to each category in the change model. Discuss each category briefly so that all team members have a good understanding of what they are rating. Table 1 gives some guidance on how to determine the score (from zero to 100) within each category. Don't worry about the precision of the numeric scores—this tool is designed to stimulate a dialogue about your readiness. Whether you rate something a *60* or a *62.35* is not nearly as important as whether your team agrees that you are prepared (or unprepared) in a particular area.

Team members can record their scores on a chart similar to the one in Figure 3.

The facilitator should sketch this chart on a whiteboard or flip chart and ask team members to give their scores in turn. Discourage discussion until all the scores are recorded, so that people don't feel pressured to change their scores.

Table 1   Guidelines for determining degrees of readiness for change.

Category	~10%	~50%	~90%
Leading change	Nobody is in charge.	Leader is pretty clear, management commitment is clear in some areas.	Clear sponsor, clear management commitment, no doubt.
Creating a shared need	Most people are happy the way things are.	Many people think we need a change.	Everybody *knows* we need a change.
Shaping a vision	What vision?	Some consensus on what is needed, but some apathy.	Everybody knows the needed outcome.
Mobilizing commitment	Joe might help someone.	We have some resources dedicated but will need more to finish.	We have all the needed dedicated resources.
Monitoring progress	Everybody has their own opinion. That's it.	We measure some things but also go by gut feeling sometimes.	We have clear metrics for every activity we are doing.
Finishing the job	Looks like a *dump and run.*	We've made some plans but have a way to go.	We're ready: pilot run, training, recognition, and so on.
Anchoring the change	Why do we have to do *anything?*	We started talking about this but haven't really finished.	We know exactly what to adjust to embed this change.

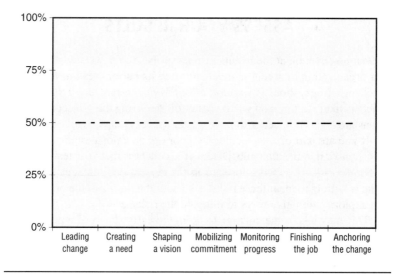

Figure 3 Score sheet for change readiness.

Taking one topic at a time, consider scores that vary by 20 points or more. Ask team members why they scored as they did. Support professional differences of opinion—a team with *all* scores in agreement is not healthy. Talk until you reach consensus on a composite score. Record this consensus score and go on to the next topic.

Apply the Two out of Three Rule

For successful initiation of a project, two of the first three categories must exceed 50 percent. *Mobilizing commitment* must always be greater than 50 percent. If any category is below 50 percent by group consensus, either take the appropriate actions or defer your project.

For example, suppose your team scored a 25 under *Shared need* because most of the organization does not currently understand the need for the change in question. You should take some actions to highlight the need, for example, holding focus groups, writing newsletter articles, and having the managers discuss it during staff meetings. Or you should reconsider the logic behind the project (maybe the organization as a whole will never support it). In either case, you will be able to make a more informed decision of how to proceed.

Later in the project, two of the last three categories must exceed 50 percent. However, they do not always need a greater than 50 percent rating at the beginning of the project. This can be developed later.

ASSESS YOUR RESULTS

Take an honest look at the results of both of these reviews: the capacity of your organization to accept more change and its current readiness to make the change in question. *If you don't pass both reviews, don't start!* Your project is likely to fail. You will be better off deferring the project until conditions are right. It is better to have a later success than an early failure.

If you are part of a project facing poor organizational readiness, bring your sponsor into the dialogue. Discuss the concerns that your team has and predict the risks of moving forward in the current environment. Ask if he or she is willing to incur these risks, ask about the timing of the project, and then explore alternative ways to mitigate the risks.

This may take some courage to do in the early stages of a project, but this is the sign of a good leader. It is better to raise concerns early than discover them after considerable time and money have been invested.

On the other hand, if your team is convinced that you are ready, you have a very good indication of where to focus your attention as the project proceeds. At this point, you will already be ahead of most projects in any companies with respect to the *human* aspects of change. Keep it up and you will be making a major contribution to your project and to your organization.

Making Change Work: A Model for Overcoming Human Resistance to Change

his chapter outlines the framework for the proper approach to the human aspects of change. This framework comprises a *change model,* a context within which the specific tools and activities take place. Figure 4 depicts the elements of the change model and the sequence in which they occur.

In the center of Figure 4, all changes move from the current state, through a transition phase, into the desired improvement state. In the beginning, it is important to create, or affirm, a broadly understood need for the change (*Creating a shared need*), along with an idea of what the outcome will look like (*Shaping a vision*). As the change effort gets underway, and throughout until the end, it must always have a sufficient amount of resources dedicated to it (*Mobilizing commitment*). As work gets completed, you must have a way to track it (*Monitoring progress*) and assure that it reaches completion (*Finishing the job*).

From the very beginning until the end, the change effort must have the backing of management and leadership from an accountable person or people (*Leading change*). At all stages, you must assure that the change will fit in the environment: the organizational structure, the business culture, the work processes, and so on. For example, if you are automating a paper-based system, you must make sure that the users will not simply keep using the old paper system. You need to address workflow changes, training and education, rewards and recognition, and transition planning, so that the new system will be aligned with the work environment.

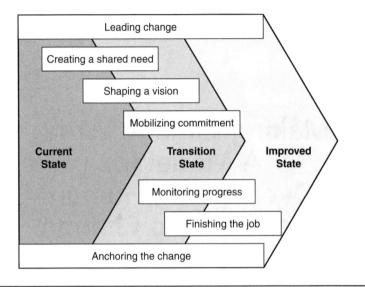

Figure 4   Change model for making change work.

For the highest assurance that a particular change will succeed, all seven steps of the change model should be in place. See Figure 5. If one area is weak, it does not necessarily portend disaster, but it does present a real risk. If you do choose to take a risk, you should do so in light of the potential consequences. These consequences are illustrated in Figure 6.

In the following chapters, the elements in the change model will be discussed in more detail and practical tools for measuring and/or implementing them will be presented. A convenient flowchart will illustrate the model, similar to the following example. In each chapter, the step being discussed will be highlighted.

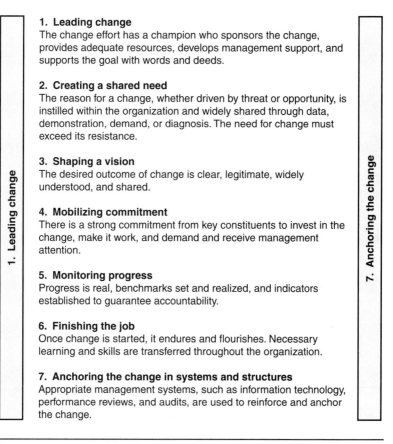

1. Leading change
The change effort has a champion who sponsors the change, provides adequate resources, develops management support, and supports the goal with words and deeds.

2. Creating a shared need
The reason for a change, whether driven by threat or opportunity, is instilled within the organization and widely shared through data, demonstration, demand, or diagnosis. The need for change must exceed its resistance.

3. Shaping a vision
The desired outcome of change is clear, legitimate, widely understood, and shared.

4. Mobilizing commitment
There is a strong commitment from key constituents to invest in the change, make it work, and demand and receive management attention.

5. Monitoring progress
Progress is real, benchmarks set and realized, and indicators established to guarantee accountability.

6. Finishing the job
Once change is started, it endures and flourishes. Necessary learning and skills are transferred throughout the organization.

7. Anchoring the change in systems and structures
Appropriate management systems, such as information technology, performance reviews, and audits, are used to reinforce and anchor the change.

Figure 5   Elements of the change model.

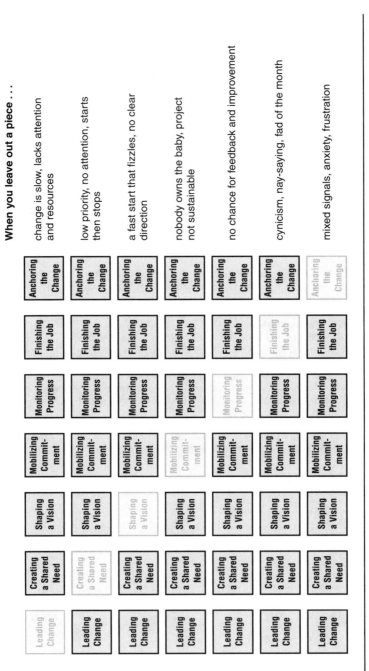

Figure 6 When you leave out a piece.

Step 1: Leading Change

As in other forms of organized human endeavor, the first step of a change initiative is to establish the leadership for it—that is, identify the people who will accept accountability for the change management actions. Without clear leadership accountability for a change project, it might never leave the talking stage.

WHY DO THIS?

Management support and communications consistently rank as the two most important success factors for changes. Strong committed leadership is critical for making change happen. Leadership impacts all other aspects of the change effort. Also, leaders must play varied roles, particularly in the different stages of the project. The team leader is the person acting as project manager, who is accountable for the outcome of the project.

During this step, there are several desired outcomes:

- Specific, identified managers are willing to give visible, active, and public commitment and support to the project.

- The sponsors and team leaders have the ability to direct resources to the project.

- The sponsors and team leaders are willing to institute leadership by example.

- The sponsors and team leaders will devote their personal focus, time, and passion.

- The team has a clear objective, scope, and set of operating norms.

If this step is not completed, there can be serious consequences:

- The change might flounder, due to lack of resources, lack of political support, or lack of alignment with the strategic priorities.

- The organization may shift to other goals before completing this change initiative.

- Leaders might delegate leadership to subordinates and fail to stay involved personally.

- The project team may fail to establish and clarify key change roles.

- The process may become diluted by too many competing initiatives and priorities.

TOOLS FOR LEADING CHANGE

Effective change leadership must build rapidly and be sustained over the entire change initiative. Four tools provide practical methodologies to assure that your project has clearly defined leadership:

- *Team charter.* Every project has an implicit scope and objective. Use a team charter to make your objectives explicit and to obtain formal written concurrence from your sponsor.

- *Calendar test.* This tool determines whether the leaders are actually putting the necessary amount of effort into the projects.

- *Personal audit.* This tool develops team members' and sponsor's awareness of what is needed for personal leadership of change efforts.

- *Adopting change roles.* This tool enables the team to assure that somebody is accountable for critical success factors.

The Team Charter

A team charter is a contract between the team and its sponsor, and among the team members themselves. It is a powerful tool that all teams should use.

There are six components of a team charter:

1. *Mission.* This section delineates the vision for the effort and its scope. It is probably the most important section and warrants careful phrasing. Team members should discuss this section in detail, so that everybody has a clear picture of the project's intention.

2. *Scope and boundaries.* This section shows the breadth of the project and whether there are any areas off-limits.

3. *Decisions.* Many teams use a consensus decision-making process to decide policy issues. If so, you should describe exactly what this means.

4. *Team roles.* Teams have special roles, aside from the normal organizational relationships. These special roles should be clearly defined.

5. *Meetings.* This section spells out some agreements in an area that can be a real problem.

6. *Ground rules.* Ground rules specify the types of behaviors that a team encourages and those that are prohibited. Spend some time on these ground rules in order to establish some professional norms *before* the pressures of the project cause bad feelings among team members.

Examples for each component are taken from a staff development team charter developed for an insurance agency that undertook an extensive effort to develop its management and staff (see sidebar, page 14).

The Calendar Test

A simple *calendar test* will help individuals and the team assess whether a sufficient investment of time is being invested in the change initiative. This test works best on projects that have been in process for a while, as a new project might not have sufficient history to determine the amount of a person's involvement.

This test is simple: check individual calendars for last 30 to 60 days to determine what percentage of time is being spent on key project-related issues and activities. This is best done as an assignment on the part of a sponsoring manager. The results are then discussed in a team meeting with the manager present.

Team Mission

The staff development team is responsible for administering systems to evaluate and develop the knowledge, skills, and abilities of all personnel (staff, management, and job candidates). These efforts will support excellent customer service, promote employee satisfaction, and assure effective recruiting practices.

Team Scope and Boundaries

The following list provides examples of items and topics that the team will focus on. (This is given for illustration; other items may be included consistent with the team's mission.)

- Developing role descriptions and competency models for all employees

- Assessing knowledge and skills of existing employees

- Planning and administering skills-development activities such as training and coaching

- Developing recruiting practices designed to attract and evaluate good candidates for employment

- Producing developmental tools such as career paths, position backups, and orientation manuals

- Tracking continuing education requirements and attendance

- Developing staffing strategies and materials

Within the scope of its mission, the team has the sole responsibility and authority to establish policy and make decisions, except as follows:

- Although team members may make recommendations regarding specific job candidates, the supervising manager always has the final right of rejection.

- Candidates for partner and department management positions require the approval of the executive team.

Continued

Decisions by Consensus

Decisions related to the team's mission will be made by consensus among the team members. Consensus decisions are characterized as follows:

- Everybody gets a chance to speak.

- Everybody is honest and does not hold back doubts or contrary opinions.

- Discussion will continue until team members reach consensus, that is, an agreement that they can live with.

- Once consensus has been reached, everybody endorses the decision, even if they might have otherwise chosen a different one themselves.

- Afterward, everyone will speak with one voice—behave as if they had personally made the decision themselves.

Team Roles

The staff development coordinator administers the day-to-day staff development responsibilities, as well as serving as team leader: coordinating team meeting times and places, maintaining the agendas, leading the meetings and keeping them on track, negotiating consensus, and facilitating the meetings.

Team members will engage in team discussions and decision making, complete agreed assignments, participate in group problem solving, and share their knowledge and experience.

Meetings

The team will meet as needed to conduct its business. As team members become aware of needs or decisions within the scope of their charter, they should identify this to the team leader in advance of the meeting. The team leader will then arrange for a meeting and put the topics on an agenda. This will give team members time to prepare. It also encourages a team approach to issues, as opposed to individuals feeling that they must do all the necessary work.

Continued

Continued

Ground Rules

Ground rules serve as a contract among team members. They describe desirable team behavior that the team promotes.

Team members agree to attend all meetings (as far as practical) and complete all assignments that they have accepted. This helps the team and also promotes the personal credibility necessary to function effectively in an organization.

Team members agree to treat other team members with respect and to recognize and appreciate the diversity of business expertise, management style, and personalities on the team.

Team members foster teamwork and continuous improvement by recognizing good work on the part of other team members.

At team meetings, one person will speak at a time, sticking to the subject at hand. Team members agree to listen actively, without interruption. Team members will speak in a professional manner, without raising their voice or using disrespectful language, and they will expect the same courtesy from other team members.

The team members will discuss a topic until either they reach consensus or they agree to address it in greater detail at the next meeting. When the team finishes discussing a topic, the team leader or another team member should summarize the decisions and/or actions agreed to before moving to the next topic. Team decisions will be recorded by the team leader or other identified person for subsequent review and validation by all team members.

In some cases, managers are surprised at how little time they spend on a project, as opposed to how dedicated they feel about it on a subjective level. In some cases, the manager may want the team to go forward even if he or she has not devoted much time toward the effort. This can lead to a delicate situation. The team leader could get caught between management direction, on one hand, and the probability of failure on the other. In these cases, the team leader should attempt to define the precise types of support needed such as money, manpower, equipment, or political backing. In other words, quantify the support needed and reach an agreement on it.

If in the end, the amount of sponsorship available is shaky or insufficient, as determined by the team leader's judgment, *now* is the time to discuss it. Don't start if the sponsor cannot or will not support the effort with personal time and involvement. There is no substitute for this level of support and almost no chance of completing the project without it. Everybody—the sponsor, the team leader, the team, the company—is better off rethinking the project at this point.

In real life, however, teams tend to avoid this sort of discussion and just go forward with silent misgivings. This is a grave mistake as the price paid is *significantly* higher at the end of a failed project than at the beginning.

If the calendar test does not bring positive results, you have two main choices:

- Look for sponsorship elsewhere such as in another affected functional area or elsewhere in the organizational hierarchy.

- Defer the project, perhaps by incorporating it into next year's strategic plans.

In any case, don't start a project without firm sponsorship, as the following example illustrates.

> At a medical device manufacturer, a team was assigned to reengineer the process for making advertising claims about a breathing apparatus in the heavily regulated medical device industry. This *claims* process extended across several departments: Marketing, Product Management, Regulatory Affairs, and Quality Assurance. Some of these departments had historically maintained uneasy relations between each other. The vice president of marketing was directed by the president to sponsor the effort.
>
> After some initial chartering meetings, the team assessed the sponsorship support and found very little calendar time spent on the part of the vice president. When the team nominated a team member to visit the sponsor and express their concern, the vice president said, "Well, just tell me what you want! I was waiting to hear from you."
>
> The team went back and quantified a modest level of support, mostly involving regular meetings with the sponsor, representing the team at executive meetings, and some small expenditures.
>
> In addition, the sponsor proposed celebrating some early achievements and held pizza and beer parties for the team members. Team members got to know each other and their sponsor. The sponsor moved from the formal corporate environment into more informal situations.
>
> This visible support sent a clear signal to the organization that this project was backed at the highest levels.

Personal Audit

The *personal audit* helps team members and sponsors judge their strengths and weaknesses with respect to change leadership. It illustrates some skills from the full range necessary to introduce change into an organization (see Table 2).

This exercise is particularly appropriate at the beginning of the project, where it can help team members begin to understand some of the human issues applicable to all projects. If this exercise strikes team members as inapplicable, then they *really* need it.

Table 2   Criteria for personal audit.

Domain	What I Do Well	What I Need to Work On
Manage attention: To what extent do I manage my time, energy, passion, focus, and agenda?		
Adopt change roles: How much attention do I pay to sponsorship issues?		
Technical competence: To what extent do I demonstrate competence in technical abilities?		
Interpersonal competence: how skilled am I at interacting with others?		
Vision: How well can I articulate the desired outcome of the project *and the benefits to others?*		
Teamwork: How often do I recognize good work done by teammates?		
Diplomacy: How closely am I working with all the groups affected by this project?		
Conflict management: Can I deal with disagreement without avoiding it or blowing up?		
Summary: Overall strengths and weaknesses		

Adopting Change Roles

Fill out a matrix similar to Table 3 to assure that you have identified specific leadership responsibilities for all of the phases and all of the roles for the change effort. Consider each aspect of the change process by reading through the workbook. In each area, indicate the sponsor, change agent (responsible party), and the people who are the target of the effort. *Sort out the change roles and identify any missing elements of effective change leadership.*

Table 3 Assigning change management roles.

Change Process	Change Sponsor	Change Agent	Change Target
1. Leading change			
2. Creating a need			
3. Shaping a vision			
4. Mobilizing commitment			
5. Monitoring progress			
6. Finishing the job			
7. Anchoring the change			

Step 2: Creating a Shared Need

The second step in any organizational change activity involves making the underlying *reason* for the change clear to everybody—team members, all of the stakeholders, and anyone affected by the project.

WHY DO THIS?

This activity creates a demonstrable need for the change—all other change activities stem from this basic *need* for change. Properly done, this step develops shared ownership by *all* the parties involved, and builds momentum needed to get the change initiative launched.

During this step, there are two desired outcomes:

- A shared recognition by both the team and the key constituents of the need for and the logic of the change.

- Confirmation among the affected parties that dissatisfaction with the status quo exceeds the cost in time, effort, money, and disruption of the change proposed.

If this step is not completed, there can be serious consequences:

- Project champions could assume that the need for change is obvious, when in fact, many people either doubt the need or are not aware of it.

21

- Failure to check for acceptance and not building true consensus among all affected parties could lead to loss of support.

- Failure to frame the need for change in a meaningful way could cause lack of buy-in, thus jeopardizing the successful implementation of the project.

- Many teams put all their focus on the technical aspects and underestimate the importance of the human aspects. Thus, an elegant technical solution could fail for lack of support, and the organization could end up worse than when the project started.

TOOLS FOR CREATING A SHARED NEED

Broad recognition of the need for change is a critical success factor. These tools provide practical methodologies to assure that the need for your project is widely understood and accepted:

1. *The cost of the status quo.* This tool identifies the total costs of the current situation. In most cases, people have come to accept the current situation over time. This tool highlights the real costs of accepting the current situation and often builds a dramatic case for doing things differently.

2. *The business case for change.* This is a very effective tool to identify concisely why the change project is important and what the desired outcome will be. The business case speaks to executives in strategic language and reinforces sponsorship of the project. Also, if the project ever slows down over time, the business case provides motivation to the affected parties.

The Cost of the Status Quo

A major problem of managing change is overcoming the inertia of the status quo. Any change makes people move out of their comfort zone, and most people will resist this. There must be a clear rationale to why the change is necessary and to why the status quo is not an option. Obviously, the disadvantages of the current state must clearly exceed the cost in time, money, effort, and risk of making the proposed change. Otherwise, why change?

It is very important to do this early on to give the change an enduring purpose and to begin building momentum. These four actions help identify the cost of the status quo:

1. Identify where the current situation does not align with the organization's mission, vision, values, and strategy.

2. Quantify the business costs of the current problem. Consider quality, money, customer satisfaction, employee satisfaction, time, and competitive pressure. Quantitative costs get real management attention.

3. Interview key stakeholders. This allows for multiple perspectives and gains a sense of ownership. Ask how the current problem impacts them. Collect stories that illustrate the actual problems experienced. Stories let everybody see how the current problem impacts others.

4. Complete surveys of the affected parties.

A midsized telecommunications company was experiencing an unintentional lack of teamwork among various departments. Everybody was performing with the best of intentions using each department's procedures, but the outcome was not meeting the needs of the vice president of operations. The vice president of human resources could see the human toll in stress and frustration and chartered a team to address the situation. He also hired a consultant to facilitate the process.

Over the course of two meetings, the consultant asked the team to brainstorm sources of frustration, prioritize these issues, and assign a cost to them. The team used the results to build a case for completing their activities based on the cost of the current situation, which had been largely hidden. The actual costs surprised all people involved, including the team members. Some of the results are shown in the example on page 24.

The Business Case for Change

Think of the change in question in the same manner as you would a major new product or business venture. If you wanted to promote a major new product or business venture to your organization, you would undoubtedly build a strong case, addressing the timing, likely returns on investment, costs, risks, and so on. You would undoubtedly think through the pros and cons, anticipate questions, consider who might object to your proposal, and decide how to respond.

In a similar manner, change advocates should build a business rationale for change and solicit input from all affected parties, *even if you have management approval for the project*. This *business case for change* should convincingly show that the risks and effects of *not* changing greatly exceed the

Where does the current situation not align with the organization's mission, vision, values, strategy, and departmental objectives:

- We "blow by" customer approval

- No review of changes for manufacturability

- Low urgency in some departments

- Production must often pull other departments

- Poor forecasts

- Bad build package completion dates

- Slow ECN and PNR approvals

- We miss dates for modem installation

- Lack of formal product specification

- Lack of respect for each department's role—due dates assigned without input

- Incorrect/incomplete documentation

- Exceeding subcontractor's capacity

- [Plus many others . . .]

Quantify the business costs of the current problem. Consider quality, money, customer satisfaction, employee satisfaction, time, and competitive pressure. Quantitative costs get real management attention.

- Items shipped without customer approval. We pay return costs, do additional work, and suffer loss of credibility.

- We can't produce item as designed, lose contract manufacturer setup time, fall behind schedule, and lose customer credibility.

- Production falls behind waiting for other departments, schedule slips, release date delays, and lost customer orders.

Continued

Continued

- Production is based on unrealistic forecasts. We scramble to make quota, work overtime, pull engineers and technicians off design work, increase stress, lose workers, and risk burnout.

- Slow engineering change document approvals hinder production, cause stress, cause work-arounds, and lead to suboptimal production and customer dissatisfaction.

- [Plus many others . . .]

(Note: Since the key stakeholders sat on the team, there was no need for interviews or surveys.)

---

costs and risks associated with changing. If they don't, you should reevaluate your plans.

The business case should present a clear logic to people in all levels of the organization. For management, it describes the rationale for the project. For the general body of employees, it explains the reasons behind the project, which is vital for gaining acceptance of the new system. And for the team, it provides an *elevator speech* to use whenever discussing the project with non–team members.

The business case should consist of a written document, one or two pages long, with any required attachments. It should address the following questions:

- What is the background for change?

- What problems are there in the current situation and what impact do they have?

- What will happen if we *don't* change?

- Why should we act *now*?

- How will we know when we have succeeded, what will the new environment look like, and how will things be different?

- What will the change require? (Be honest—point out the work required.)

- What is the cost of changing versus the cost of staying the same?

Early in the project, the team leader should outline the business case with the team, using the rules of brainstorming shown in Figure 7. Where possible, the team should quantify the costs associated with the problems by translating them into dollars, man-hours, rework, and so on.

Poll department managers not represented on the team. People generally talk freely about problems they have getting their work done. It pays to involve everyone you can.

When you are finished, write up the results, preferably on one page, and add supporting data as attachments. Review it with the sponsor. Ask the sponsor or other key executive to publicize this business case at a company-wide employee meeting, in the company newsletter, in a mass e-mailing, or similar vehicle.

You should refer to the business case frequently, as it contains the essence of the project: rationale, current *pain*, desired outcome, and impact of the work. The business case for change will keep team members and management focused if support starts to lag.

Two examples illustrate the scope of application of these tools. The first example is a strategic planning project for a fast-growing, formerly rural community on the outskirts of a major metropolitan area. The team presented some elements in the business case orally (background, current situation) to keep the document brief. The business case led the municipal council to charter a strategic planning effort that included the council, the mayor, the administrative staff, and the presidents of the local boards and commissions.

A business case can actually survive the demise of a project and lead to its later resurrection and completion. A successful financial services

---

Rules of Brainstorming:

- Announce the subject of the brainstorming, for example, "Now let's list some of the problems that we are experiencing."
- Everybody gets a chance to shout out something. Write everything down—*no discussion.*
- Assure that everybody gets a chance to speak. (Perhaps query everybody in turn.)
- When the ideas have died down, review the list and combine the duplicates.
- Using consensus, prioritize the list. (Encourage discussion at this point.)
- With the team's consent, drop items that few people support.

Figure 7   Rules of brainstorming.

The Business Case for Developing a Mission, Vision, and Strategic Plan for the Municipality

Proposal

Develop a formal mission, vision, and strategic plan covering all aspects of municipal government activities.

Why Should We Do This?

- We have many activities in progress—the comprehensive plan, the park acquisition, [others]—and we need to include them all into a master plan to assure the appropriate use of resources.

- We need to have clear priorities, milestones, and leaders for all municipal projects and activities.

- We need a clear alignment of all aspects of municipal government with an agreed mission, long-term vision, and strategic plans.

- We need to weigh the needs and desires of all stakeholders using a fair and open process to give everyone input and to assure ongoing faith in the municipal government.

- We need to assure continuity over the long term to allow appropriate completion of projects that last longer than the elected or appointed terms in office of government officials.

What If We Don't Do This?

- We will take on too much and fail to complete some things.

- We will not have clear priorities agreed to by all constituents.

- We will have perceptions of pet projects.

- We may not have clear accountabilities for all projects and activities.

- Citizens and businesses may start to lose faith in the managerial abilities of the municipal government.

Continued

Continued

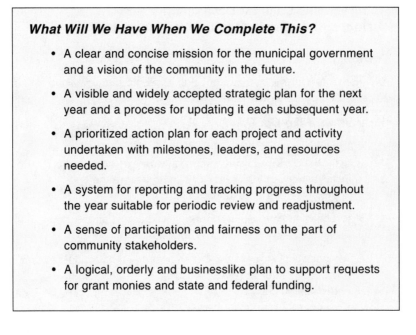

What Will We Have When We Complete This?

- A clear and concise mission for the municipal government and a vision of the community in the future.

- A visible and widely accepted strategic plan for the next year and a process for updating it each subsequent year.

- A prioritized action plan for each project and activity undertaken with milestones, leaders, and resources needed.

- A system for reporting and tracking progress throughout the year suitable for periodic review and readjustment.

- A sense of participation and fairness on the part of community stakeholders.

- A logical, orderly and businesslike plan to support requests for grant monies and state and federal funding.

company transitioned ownership from the founder to a business partnership owned by the employees. Although the company kept growing, it did not develop the leadership and management systems necessary to support its growth. Also, the culture suffered from some bad practices originated by the founder. The business case shown on page 29 documents the reasons for changing the current practice.

After a year or so, the project floundered and eventually came to a halt. The company chose to install a major technological system to avoid Y2K problems, and most money and management resources were deferred to this system installation. In the meantime, they experienced quality problems and lost customers, causing cash flow problems and exacerbating the situation even more.

After nearly three years and much frustration, the chief operating officer gathered his management team together and reviewed the current situation. "Look what we said," he told the team, pointing at the business case and looking around. "We said we'd lose customers, and we did. We said we'd be more disorganized, and we are. We said our reputation would suffer, and it has. Everything that we said would happen *is* happening.

"We need to get on track and hold ourselves responsible for finishing this. Now, I am probably the person most responsible for letting this project

The Business Case for Change

Why We Need to Change

- The current situation is not meeting our expectations.
- We are starting to experience problems related to quality and customer satisfaction.
- We don't have a long-range strategy, business plans, or goals.
- We are not providing our people with sufficient training, recognition, and management support.
- We have inconsistent work processes, particularly between different offices.
- Managers and employees are expressing frustration.
- These problems are limiting our ability to grow and may hurt the long-term value of the company.

What If We Fail to Act

- We will face more disorganization in the future.
- We stand a very good chance of losing business clients.
- We may end up with fewer satisfied clients.
- We face potential legal liabilities.
- Our reputation may suffer, causing further damage to business.
- We will lose good employees through turnover.

What the New Environment Will Look Like

- Defined lines of authority, accountability, and responsibility of all levels in the organization.
- Structure in policies and procedures so that employees know what they are expected to do, adequate training to show them how to do their job, and support to allow them to function successfully and provide recognition by peers and management.

Continued

Continued

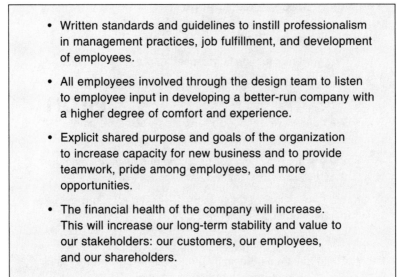

- Written standards and guidelines to instill professionalism in management practices, job fulfillment, and development of employees.

- All employees involved through the design team to listen to employee input in developing a better-run company with a higher degree of comfort and experience.

- Explicit shared purpose and goals of the organization to increase capacity for new business and to provide teamwork, pride among employees, and more opportunities.

- The financial health of the company will increase. This will increase our long-term stability and value to our stakeholders: our customers, our employees, and our shareholders.

stop earlier. I am totally committed to making it happen this time. Are you with me?" With that, the team rechartered and went to work. Within two months, they had achieved the quickest and most consistent cycle times in the company's history. Employee morale and company profit rose dramatically, and the company had a new lease on life.

Step 3: Shaping a Vision

After people have agreed on the need to make a change, they need to envision what the outcome of the change will look like. This picture—the "vision"—provides a map toward the desired outcome.

WHY DO THIS?

Vision paints a picture that appeals to both head and heart. By this time in the change effort, participants are well aware of the problems and the need for change. If they lack a clear picture of how the future will look, they might overfocus on the problems and not see the possibility for change. A vision of the desired end helps people focus on solutions, rather than just on the problems.

A clear statement of the future state helps gain genuine commitment, establishes milestones, and changes system and structures.

During this step, there are two desired outcomes:

- A clear picture of the outcome of the change effort.

- A view of the future state that is:

  - Customer focused

  - Challenging

  - Easy to understand

- Not just one person's dream

- Evolving, not static

- Behavioral and actionable

If this step is not completed, there can be serious consequences:

- People might not understand the outcome, and so may not plan for or support it.

- Everyone could have has his or her own idea of what is desired.

- The vision could be too lofty or too complex.

- The vision could change too often with time and never get *traction*.

TOOLS FOR SHAPING A VISION

Stating the vision in actionable, behavioral terms helps the team gain commitment and identify sources of resistance. These tools provide practical methodologies to assure that the outcome that your project is designed to achieve is widely understood and accepted:

1. *Describing success.* This exercise helps put some specificity to the results of the project.

2. *Key phrases exercise.* This exercise helps develop a common language for use in describing the project. This allows team members to give a consistent message to the rest of the organization.

3. *More of/less of exercise.* This easy and helpful exercise helps the team define the future by explaining what will be different.

4. *Elevator speech.* The elevator speech helps the team articulate their charter quickly and consistently.

All of these exercises are designed to develop a vision of success on the team members' part. In turn, team members can articulate the desired outcomes to other people, helping to align the organization's thinking toward this end.

Describing Success

In a team meeting, ask participants to imagine a point in the future when the project has been very successful. Invite team members to describe what they hear, see, and feel in the new changed state. Describe how people's daily activities are different. Write this input on a flip chart or whiteboard.

Start free-form, using the rules of brainstorming (see Figure 7, page 26). After a while, stop and look at the list. Discuss it until the team forms a consensus on how the future state ought to look.

Test this description on others, particularly managers, customers, and other stakeholders who cannot be present. See whether it moves them and addresses real needs. Modify it as required based on their input.

Encourage team members to remember this exercise and use the results to describe the desired outcome to other people. The following example illustrates this process.

Key Phrases Exercise

Shared visions come from collective efforts that reflect individual perspectives. Ask team members individually to jot down key phrases that capture

A manufacturing company decided to adopt a policy of shipping orders within 24 business hours of receiving an order. This commitment required that the customer service, shipping, and accounting department managers work as a team—for the first time. It would also require the integration of the separate processes for order entry, picking and packing, and accounts receivable.

The team of managers initially spent much time on details without coming to any agreement on an integrated approach. After several meetings, they invited a facilitator to attend. He suggested that the team define the end point, or objective. "That's easy," said one of the managers. "We are supposed to ship 95 percent of the orders within 24 hours." The facilitator asked, "So, if we ship within 24 hours, what has to happen?" Team members then started talking about the sequence of order entry, stock picking, and so on. By the end of the meeting, they agreed to return the next week with a clear explanation of how each department's activities would have to work to support the goal of 24-hour shipment. From that point on, the team members focused their efforts in working backward from the 24-hour shipment outcome.

They tried many changes to the overall process, and over time they were able to raise the percentage of 24-hour shipments to the 95 percent range.

the essence of why the team exists, the need it addresses, and the goal of the team. Address the desired outcomes as follows: "We'll know our work is done when . . ."

Collect and collate these phrases, and discuss them. Write them into a simple mission statement for the team. Test this statement with the sponsor, key customers, and other affected parties. Modify it as necessary.

When you have the concurrence of the team and its sponsor, ask team members to use these key phrases in conversations with other people in the organization. Consider using them in communications such as newsletter articles or management updates, as illustrated in the following example.

More of/Less of Exercise

In a team meeting, explain that you are going to draw out from the team a clearer picture of the environment after the project has been successfully completed. Draw two columns on a bulletin board or flip chart as

At a nuclear power plant, an audit discovered that the organization had more than 40 forms used to report situations that did not meet requirements: nonconformance reports, condition reports, work requests, audit findings, corrective action reports, maintenance requests, and so on. Most of these reports used a similar process to report a problem in a different area or operation of the plant.

An operations team was assembled to consolidate, simplify, and streamline these processes. Members set as a goal the consolidation of all of these forms into a single, multipurpose form. To emphasize the goal, the team created a name for the new form: the Operations Notification and Evaluation Form, or ONE Form. The ONE Form caught on because of its double meaning, and set the tone for the project. The idea of a single form to replace multiple forms was an easily understood objective.

To publicize the form, the team decided to encourage its widespread use. People were asked to fill ONE out if they *thought* there was a problem. Accordingly, the team created a tag line for use in training: "When in doubt, fill one out." This also caught on, and made the system user-friendly and accepted by the employees, even though it represented a significant shift from the previous use of multiple forms.

More of:	Less of:
• Use of computerized drawing databases	• Complaints about late drawings
•	•
•	•
•	•
•	•

Figure 8 More of/less of exercise.

shown in Figure 8. Summarize the project's mission and vision. If you have done a business case for change, refer back to it.

Ask team members to identify *specific measurable behaviors* they expect to see more of or less of when the project is successfully completed. Use the rules of brainstorming to generate ideas. Then review the lists, negotiate the individual entries, and put them in order of significance.

After you have reached a consensus, validate the *more of/less of* list by presenting it to others outside the team including the sponsor. Ideally, you should do this before attempting to win support of the key stakeholders. That way, you can have a very convincing case for the project: it will involve more good stuff and less pain! This may not remove all skepticism, but it surely will focus everyone on the desired outcomes and the benefits of the future instead of the pain of today. *Clarify what the team expects from the new state in behavioral terms.* An example of an effective more of/less of exercise is shown in the example on page 36.

The Elevator Speech

In a team meeting, explain to team members that they are going to create a short, uniform description of the project that they will use in discussing the project with interested parties.

Ask them to imagine meeting a key executive in an empty elevator with just a few floors to ride. The executive says, "I hear that you are working on a new project. What's going on with it?" The team member has only about a minute to discuss the project. Naturally, he or she wants to make a good impression, get the executive nodding in agreement, and even start the executive thinking about how to help. The *elevator speech* does all of this.

A manufacturer and distributor of medical devices assigned an employee to contact leads from trade shows. The employee discovered that there was no system in place to do so. Show attendees came back to the office with shoe boxes of forms that prospects had completed and set them on a desk. In one case, a show had cost several hundred thousand dollars in time, travel expenses, and show materials and had not resulted in one fulfilled lead!

In addition, the company had no uniform way to answer incoming inquiries about the products. Calls got routed by happenstance, and customers were not happy.

The vice president of sales commissioned a team to design a system to manage and close sales leads and to turn inquiries into sales. The team set its goals based on the problems it had found to date and the desired outcomes.

More of/Less of Exercise

More of	**Less of**
• Completed and legible follow-up forms	• Illegible forms
• Prompt follow-up	• Delinquent or missing follow-up
• Metrics on sales from trade shows	• Uncertain sales results from shows
• Uniform system for all follow-ups and telephone inquiries	• Different business practices for each product line
• One person managing all inquiries	• Shuttling inquiries to several people
• Inquiries treated as sales prospects	• Inquiries treated as interruptions

To develop this speech, ask team members to consider the following format, one line at a time. For each line, write down team members' suggestions.

"We found that there is a real problem with _____,
    especially how it is hurting the company."

"If we don't do anything about it, _____ will happen."

"We have a group of people from all the affected areas and we
    decided that we need _____."

"If you are interested, we could use your help in _____."

When you have finished, circle the suggestion that the team considers the best. Don't worry about the exact wording, just capture the gist of the topic.

Then comes the important part: practice. Team members should practice this speech, so they can convey a uniform message to others. Starting with an extroverted person, have him or her to say the 60-second speech in their own words. Then ask other team members how they liked it. You can kid around a little, so people feel better about taking their turn.

Go around the room until everybody has a chance to articulate the elevator speech. Try to get everyone involved but don't press too hard. If someone does not want to take a turn, ask, "Are you comfortable with this?"

After the meeting, team members should use this elevator speech whenever they talk to other people about the project. This makes sure that the team presents a clear, consistent message about the vision of the project. *Communicating a clear purpose helps overcome apathy. People appreciate this and are more likely to support you,* as shown in the following example.

As a nuclear power plant ended its construction phase, the engineering manager wanted to develop a set of operating procedures unique to the site, rather than relying on the standard and rather cumbersome procedures used by the parent corporation. This was a major effort, which at other facilities had involved more than 6,000 procedures.

The project faced some known resistance. Local managers worried that the program would be too heavily influenced by the corporate representatives and thus too bureaucratic. The engineering manager wanted to make a fresh start, creating efficient, integrated, user-centered work processes. Corporate managers worried that the effort would not comply with previous commitments made to federal regulators.

The team chartered to develop the procedures decided at an early stage to stress both the efficiency and the compliance goals

---

Continued

Continued

in order to appeal to both sets of stakeholders. Early on, they developed this standard characterization of the project:

> We are developing brand new, user-oriented work processes that will clearly comply with regulatory requirements while serving the needs of the users. We plan to have the most efficient operations and best regulatory record in the system.

The consistent theme helped generate a positive atmosphere at the site and at the corporate headquarters, and helped gain buy-in for the managers who needed to approve the procedures.

Step 4: Mobilizing Commitment

For any business initiative to work, it must have sufficient resources assigned to it. Furthermore, it must avoid a build-up of opposition from the organization, which could slow the project or cause it to stop completely. This step will provide tools to measure and build commitment, and to mitigate the natural human tendency to resist change.

WHY DO THIS?

Regardless of its technical justification, any change effort needs sufficient support and involvement from key stakeholders. The ability to mobilize commitment often makes the difference between a success and a good idea that failed.

All projects—in fact, all change—will encounter resistance from those affected by it. This is a normal fact of human behavior. Instead of denying resistance, or ignoring it, it is far better to expect it, allow its healthy expression, and convert the stakeholders—through logic, communication, and involvement—from uncertain resistors to clear advocates of the change needed.

During this step, there are three desired outcomes:

- Identify and convert key influence agents.

- Identify the sources of possible resistance and plan how to react.

- Obtain a coalition of committed supporters.

If this step is not completed, there can be serious consequences:

- Project participants and sponsors might assume that a technical solution is sufficient, and risk foundering on the shoals of organizational resistance.

- Technically oriented project members may fail to anticipate and manage the inevitable organizational resistance, putting the project at risk.

- Project personnel may not involve others due to time constraints and/or lack of understanding, thus jeopardizing the acceptance of the change.

- Lack of political sensitivity may blindside team members and bring the project to a halt.

TOOLS FOR MOBILIZING COMMITMENT

For a change to succeed, a critical mass of people must *be won over.* These tools provide practical methodologies to develop commitment for the change effort you are putting in place:

1. *Understanding and managing resistance.* Use this tool to enable team members to understand the nature of human reaction to change, and plan for "bumps in the road" as the project proceeds.

2. *Key constituents map.* Use this tool to review who will be impacted by the change.

3. *Stakeholders analysis.* Use this tool to identify who is "for" and "against" the project, and how to gain the needed support.

4. *Technical–political–cultural analysis.* Identify sources of resistance and the roots of this resistance with this tool.

5. *Developing an influence strategy.* Use this exercise to develop a plan to win converts and assuage the organizational resistance to the change.

6. *Resolving differences and conflict.* Manage professional differences of opinion, which can lead to conflict, with a step-by-step process. Use it to develop win–win outcomes for differences of opinion.

7. *Communicating the need for change.* Use this tool to plan how to get the word out about the project. Every significant change effort should have a detailed strategy for communications.

Understanding and Managing Resistance

When we raise objections to proposed changes, we call it realistic thinking. When other people raise objections to the changes we endorse, we call it resistance.

In general, people do try to maintain the status quo, which gives organizations continuity through time. From a pragmatic perspective, you should understand that *all* change brings resistance. This knowledge lets you anticipate resistance and mitigate it.

In fact, people do not so much resist *change* as they resist *being changed.* Your job is to involve people from the beginning to build the business case for change and to communicate how people will be affected. Change is much better accepted if people feel that they have some control and understanding, and that the change has a good purpose: either their lives will be made easier or the business as a whole will benefit.

Since resistance is inevitable, you should acknowledge it openly. Ask for doubts and criticisms and don't try to negate them. Acknowledge them and take them into consideration. It is far healthier to discuss professional concerns in the open, rather than driving the discussions underground. In a similar vein, don't try to minimize the cost and effort that the proposed change will require.

As a general of rule of thumb, some 25 percent of an organization will actively support a reasonable change effort; these people are ideal to have on the implementation teams, providing they have the required expertise. Recognize these individuals and reinforce their behavior.

A majority of people—roughly 50 percent—will start out neutral, and take a *wait-and-see* attitude. They can end up either supporting the change or opposing it. This group warrants the most attention on the part of the change team. They need to become more and more convinced until the change effort reaches an intangible *tipping point*, and the momentum clearly supports completing the change. If this does not occur, the majority could oppose the change and provide sufficient inertia to cause the project to fail.

There will also be a minority of about 25 percent that actively opposes the change. They too must be dealt with because they can sway an uncommitted majority, or they might actively work to thwart the team's good intentions. The best way to communicate is through honest dialogue. In the end, though, recognize that not everybody will come to support the change. *Spend most of the time convincing the neutral majority, not the skeptical minority.*

Key Constituents Map

This exercise identifies key clusters of constituents who will be impacted by the change initiative as well as their relative levels of interest and involvement. This works best if started at a high level with broad groups. This can help a team broaden its perspective regarding who the constituents are, where they reside in the organization, and what their relative size is.

In a team meeting, consider the impact of the change on the major functional areas in your organization, such as Engineering, Human Resources, Manufacturing, and Finance. (See Figure 9.) You will want to customize this list based on your own organization. For this exercise, it pays to think like a devil's advocate; that is, consider *any* impact, even if favorable.

Use this low-risk activity to set the stage for future discussions on building a constituency for change. *This provides a pictorial representation of the groups that must be won over for change to be successful.*

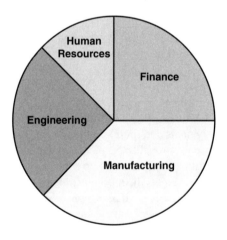

Figure 9   Key constituents map.

Stakeholder Analysis for Change

In a team meeting, use this tool to understand the current political environment and identify where further action is required. A chart similar to Table 4 will help visualize team input.

Consider the affected departments and address the following questions:

- Who are the stakeholders? Who controls resources? Who can block the change, directly or indirectly? Who must approve aspects of the change? Who owns the process? Who are the thought leaders?

- How does the stakeholder view the merits of the change initiative? (List the estimated level of support, with a *5* indicating strong support, *3* indicating neutrality, and *1* indicating strong opposition.)

- How critical is each person's support to the success of the project? (Use the same scale, with *5* indicating that the person's support is vital, and *1* indicating a low level of criticality.)

- What is the level of attention needed for each person? Based on discussion, rank levels as *high, medium,* or *low.* In general, a stakeholder with a low current acceptance of the effort and a high degree of criticality warrants a high level of attention; whereas someone with low criticality and high acceptance warrants less.

With this information, particularly in connection with the subsequent tools, you can build an influence strategy for assuring the success of the project in the political dimension. For example, strong cynics with high criticality warrant a lot of attention, as you try to understand their opposition and turn this into support. Strong supporters require recognition and involvement to keep their support strong. And in some cases, all you want is a neutral person to remain neutral.

Table 4   Stakeholder analysis.

Department	Key Stakeholder	Current Acceptance	Criticality to project	Level of attention needed

While this evaluation of the political environment may seem distasteful to some people, particularly technical people, it is absolutely essential on a pragmatic level. Like it or not, office politics usually trumps technical expertise. It is better to be technically correct *and* successful than to be correct but dead in the water. An example of a successful use of this tool follows.

Technical–Political–Cultural Analysis

In a team meeting, complete this tool to understand the nature of resistance that key stakeholders might be showing. Use a table similar to Table 5 to record your data.

A nuclear power plant under construction got into trouble with federal regulators. Work stopped while the owners responded to federal and civil lawsuits alleging impropriety.

It became clear that the only feasible route was to perform massive reinspections and engineering evaluations of the completed work in a critical and closely monitored environment. The reinspection teams, who were not involved in the original construction, tended to resent the close overviews of their work.

As a result, the team of outside consultants hired to overview the teams used this tool to identify the key players and to attempt to reconcile their concerns. After a series of discussions—and after some managers had to testify in court—team members came to appreciate the need for overview and validation of their work.

Department	Key Stakeholder	Current Acceptance	Criticality to Project	Level of Attention Needed
Engineering	Manager	1	High	Very high
Engineering	Electrical group leader	3	Medium	Medium
Engineering	Mechanical group leader	1	Medium	High
Engineering	Civil group leader	2	Medium	Medium high
Quality Assurance	Manager	5	High	Low

Table 5 Technical–political–cultural analysis.

Sources of Resistance	Definition of Resistance	Examples	Percent
Technical			
Political			
Cultural			

Total = 100%

Consider each of the affected departments, especially where acceptance is low and importance is high. Classify the nature of the resistance, based on the team's best judgment, according to these three criteria:

- *Technical.* Costs required, lack of skills available, lack of critical resources, doubt as to outcome, and so on.

- *Political.* Issues of power, authority, and relationships.

- *Cultural.* Norms, mind-sets, habits, and such.

Use this tool to understand the nature of resistance prior to developing customized pitches addressing each group's issues and concerns. For example, don't spend time arguing the technical virtues of the change if most of resistance is in the cultural realm.

As with all negotiations, it is better to avoid a win/lose situation, in which, for example, the team's gain is a department manager's loss. It is better to turn resistance into a win/win situation. To do this, you must understand the reasons underlying someone's resistance and find a way to preserve what you want to do *and* avoid the negative outcome that worries them. (Tool 6, resolving conflicts and differences, futher explains how to do this).

For example, if after using this tool, you find that a person or department worries that your project will not work (a technical concern), you must demonstrate that it will. Share your data with them, acknowledge their concern, and try to make them as confident as you are.

If the concern is political, you might want to arrange a high-level discussion between managers. Usually political concerns relate to loss of *turf*. You can usually assuage these concerns if you are clear about your intentions and demonstrate that you have no intention to encroach on their turf. By reading the example on page 46, you should have a better understanding of the nature of resistance.

At a technology company, the president's assistant was assigned to manage the installation of a corporate e-mail system. The manager assembled a team that included representatives from several departments, hoping to gain buy-in from them. However, the installation encountered much resistance throughout the organization.

The team spent several meetings attempting to understand the nature of resistance but failed to make progress. The team was getting discouraged that such a seemingly straightforward project was getting waylaid before it really got started.

Finally, the team analyzed the specifics of the objections offered by the different departments. This exercise showed that there were some very different types of countervailing views, as shown. Given a more specific understanding of what different departments thought, the team was able to address them directly.

Engineering

Sources of Resistance	Definition of Resistance	Examples	Percent
Technical	Feeling of lack of ability to make technical input	Manager's objections	100%
Political	N/A	N/A	0
Cultural	N/A	N/A	0

Administrative

Sources of Resistance	Definition of Resistance	Examples	Percent
Technical	N/A	N/A	0
Political	Fear of excessive bureaucracy; lack of trust of IT department	Complaints about treatment during previous projects	80%
Cultural	Uncertainty about using new technology, especially with insufficient training	Slow adaptation of previous order entry system	20%

Developing an Influence Strategy

This exercise is most effectively completed in connection with the previous two. You should complete this for each stakeholder whose influence is important to the project. Even stakeholders that are already *moderately* or *strongly* supportive may have issues that need to be addressed.

List the affected stakeholders and record their main issues and concerns in a table similar to Table 6. Determine how their concerns can be addressed without sidetracking the project. Here are some considerations in doing this:

- What are the real, underlying issues? Can we address them?

- What history needs to be considered?

- If the stakeholder is entrenched, can we create a resolution that will let them save face?

- What is the stakeholder's style?

- How is the stakeholder best approached (one-on-one, informally, demo, or other way)?

- Who can best influence the stakeholder?

Use the results of this exercise to plan your action, as illustrated in the following example. Manage all of these actions just as you would any other project action item: schedule and assign them, track them, report completion, and so forth.

It these actions fail to win over supporters, use Tool 6, resolving differences and conflict.

Table 6   Developing influence strategies.

Stakeholder	Issues/Concerns	Influence

During an e-mail installation project (discussed on page 46), the team had identified two sources of opposition to the project. The engineering department had some technical opinions that they felt were not being considered by the information systems (IS) manager on the team. The IS manager was open to input but had not realized that Engineering had any interest in the specific technology to be selected.

From the administrative and customer service staff, the team saw reluctance with a very different origin. They had a bad experience in a previous software installation run by another IS manager. Based on this previous experience, they feared that the team would ramrod a new system without any feedback. Also, they were concerned that they would be mandated to use a new system without prior training.

The team used this exercise to determine how to address the objections of the departments in question, reconciling their legitimate concerns with the objectives of the team. They developed an understanding of the different points of view, discussed the best response, and assigned team members to approach the managers.

Stakeholder	Issues/Concerns	Influence
Engineering manager	Technical adequacy	Offer to put representative on team. [Name] to approach manager in private.
Administrative manager	1. Fears lack of input, based on previous system installation 2. Lack of training before implementation	1. Invite on team 2. Offer training 3. Offer to use department for pilot run. Iron out any problems noted. Gain influence on project. 4. [Name 2] to approach manager, invite to next meeting.

It turns out that the team was quite correct in its assessment of the sources of objections. Since the team members approached the managers with each manager's concerns in mind, rather than trying to promote only the team's needs, the managers were quite receptive. Both accepted the offers of the team, and both contributed staff members to join the team.

With a better understanding of the source and the nature of the objections to the project, the team members were able to take action to assure its successful completion.

Resolving Differences and Conflict

This process applies to negotiating in general. With respect to change management, it provides good guidelines for talking to an important but resistant stakeholder. It is designed to preserve the legitimate interests of both parties and move past apparently intransigent positions.

Follow this process in order. Focus strictly on the business issues on hand. Say nothing about the other person or their motives, but it is okay and healthy to say how *you* feel.

Understand the Other Person's Position

Without having to agree with the other person, ask the stakeholder about his or her position. Ask what led to that position. Confirm your understanding by repeating his or her position. Don't argue and don't disagree, just try to understand.

Explain Your Position

After you are sure that you do understand the other person's position, explain your position. Explain why you feel as you do. Check for the stakeholder's understanding of your position. Ask them if he or she can see the logic in your position even if he or she still disagrees with your conclusion. Say, "I'm not trying to convince you here. I'm just trying to make sure that you understand me."

Seek Common Ground

Confirm your big picture agreements. For example, you can say, "We both obviously want what is best for the organization," or "We both do agree that there are problems with the current situation."

Find more detailed common ground. Systematically examine all areas of agreement, and then set them aside. Confirm your understanding. For example: "It looks like we agree on A, B, and C. The only area that we still don't agree on is D. Right?"

This is very important: focus on the areas of agreement first, even if it is tempting to focus on areas of disagreement. Often both sides come to realize how narrow their differences really are and tend to be more comfortable with the other's position.

If You Still Disagree, Try Another Tactic

Attempt to set standards for investigating past data. For example: "I'll tell you what. Let's do some research and check X. If we find that A is true, I'll agree with you. If we find that B is true, will you agree with me?"

Set up an experiment or pilot run. Discuss the issue further based on the results.

Accept one solution provisionally. Agree on a set of measurements. Set a date for a review, and then examine the evidence. For example: "Let's just try this for three months, and then regroup. If it works out like I think, we'll continue doing it the way I advocate. If it works out like you think, then we'll do it the other way."

Ask for some outside input from a respected third party. For really intractable problems, you might suggest binding arbitration, in which a third party will render a decision that both other parties agree to abide with.

Most disagreements really involve a failure to hear the other party's position. Not feeling understood, both parties resist the other's position with the equivalent of brute force. This ends up somewhat like a rugby scrum, where each side pushes as hard as they can, and a lot of energy is expended with little movement of the ball.

This tool starts from a position of understanding, thus avoiding the intransigence often seen otherwise. Reasonable people find it hard to resist a person who honestly wants to hear and respect their legitimate professional opinion. The quickest way to enlist a supporter is to demonstrate this respect, as shown in the following example.

At a high-tech manufacturing company, a team was chartered to install a company intranet, install a new e-mail system, and to migrate some engineering records transmittals from paper-based to electronic. Early on, the team realized that the R&D engineers were resisting the team's direction, and it invited some engineers to a discussion.

Using a facilitator, team members explained their objectives and listened carefully to the engineers' concerns. It turns out that their concerns involved two issues: the choice of the e-mailing system software and the security of the engineering records to be transmitted via e-mail.

By *peeling the onion,* the team was able to demonstrate the adequacy of their choice of systems. Also, they were able to acknowledge the concern for records security and design the appropriate safeguards. The engineers were satisfied after this discussion and changed their opposition to support.

To assure the engineers' continuing support, they resorted to the ultimate negotiating tool: they invited one of them to serve on the team. This not only helped smooth organizational resistance but also added a strong technical strength as well.

Communicate Effectively

Communications and management support consistently rank as the two most important success factors for changes. Most teams managing change report that they should have communicated more often, with 75 percent recommending communications at least weekly. Use the following guidelines to design an effective communications plan. The success of your effort depends on it!

- *Select the audience.* Review communication tools.

- *Determine the goals of communication* for each audience:

  - Inform

  - Persuade

  - Listen to objections

  - Ask for help

- *Points to communicate:*

  - These are problems and related costs with the current situation.

  - This will happen if we *don't* change.

  - The new system will do this for us.

  - Here is what the change requires.

  - We need your help and cooperation.

  - We appreciate everybody's efforts.

- *Determine the logistics:*

  - *Vehicles.* All-employee meetings, staff meetings, newsletter, memos, bulletin boards, e-mails, and voice mail.

  - *Frequency.* Keep the effort visible.

Early and continuous communication is essential.

A financial services company spent a tremendous amount of time and money installing a software system and mitigating legacy system issues related to Y2K. As a result, resources were drawn from customer service functions, quality suffered, some customers left, and employee morale declined. When the computer project ended, the executives wanted to refocus on customer service, teamwork, and some important leadership issues. The executives drafted the letter shown on page 52 to announce this effort to all employees.

To: All employees
From: Executive team
Subject: Teamwork and customer service

Employee meetings were recently held to inform all employees of the formation of a Teamwork and Customer Service (TCS) Team. The following is a summary of the items that were discussed.

As you all know, during the last couple of years a lot of emphasis has been put on developing our new computer system. We have one more major component to add to the system. From there, we would expect to fine-tune the system and add enhancements, which will not only assist all employees in doing their jobs but will also provide us with the ability to improve our customer service.

Unfortunately, during this development, we have spent too little time in developing our employees, which are the company's most meaningful assets. What we have learned during the last several years is that the company lacked organization and focus. At the same time, we have learned that for the most part, the core of the company—the employees—are dedicated, resourceful, and dependable, and have a desire to promote not only themselves as individuals but the company as a whole.

Just as with the computer system, we acknowledge that we must provide our employees with organization, training, and recognition in order to fine-tune and enhance our employees' ability to meet the company's primary objective, being recognized as the best third-party administrator.

We are in the process of doing just that.

First, we have established a Teamwork and Customer Service Team. The team leader is _____, chief operations officer. The other team members are:

[List of names and titles]

The team's mission is to create a productive environment in which all employees work together to accomplish the company's goal of total customer satisfaction.

The team will focus on company operations and employee development. To do so, the team will need to define and document job descriptions for all employees, define and document all workflows, and develop appropriate written procedures. We will also

Continued

Continued

need to identify and make all employees aware of their external and internal customers, provide proper training to all employees in all areas that affect their ability to perform (telephone etiquette, e-mail, voice mail, Word, Excel, etc.). Last but not least, we will be establishing employee recognition programs to acknowledge and reward superior performance.

As stated earlier, we believe that the company's most valuable assets are its employees. Therefore, all employees will have the opportunity to participate in the development of these projects, especially in the areas of role descriptions and work processes. We believe that each employee has the ability to provide valuable input as to the most efficient and effective means of performing his/her daily functions.

We believe that these efforts will provide all employees with an environment that promotes individual self-esteem and value, as well as meeting or exceeding company goals.

Although this is a major project, and it will take time and additional effort from everyone, we are committed to seeing this project through to its completion.

In the meantime, we wish to thank all employees for your efforts to date and your cooperation and additional efforts in the future.

Step 5: Monitoring Progress

This chapter discusses tools useful for providing feedback on the progress and the success of the change initiative. These tools enable project leaders to measure progress and take corrective actions where necessary.

WHY DO THIS?

All projects require accurate measuring and tracking systems. They provide focus, direction, and momentum for the team. Also, corrective action can only occur when you know you're off track.

Use the first tool to design project-specific measurements. Use the second and third tools to evaluate the likelihood of success of the project itself.

During this step, there are three desired outcomes:

- Gain agreement and understanding on what the change effort will produce, and, in measurable and observable terms, when.

- Assure that baseline date and milestone results are tracked and widely shared.

- Increase the momentum as people see progress and results.

If this step is not completed, there can be serious consequences:

- You will not know whether you are on track.

- The project could seem infinite to your sponsors, and they might pull the plug.

- Other stakeholders may lose interest.

- Your team might flounder, with no end in sight.

- You will not compare well with other projects and may lose executive attention.

TOOLS FOR MONITORING PROGRESS

A good measurement system can make the difference between a hit or a miss. These tools provide practical methodologies to track your project:

1. *Checkpoints for a good measuring system.* Use this tool's guidelines for good project management practices.

2. *Change process profile.* Use this tool to make sure that your change management activities stay on track.

3. *Force-field analysis.* Use this to analyze the forces working toward your success and the forces working against you.

Checkpoints for Measurement Systems

Use this tool at any point in the project to assure that you have an adequate system in place to measure progress. For each milestone, assure that you have clear *deliverables* identified and that individual accountabilities are specified.

When you are satisfied with your progress measuring system, regularly send the stakeholders *concise,* one-page reports. This keeps progress evident and prevents you from falling under the radar of management attention. There are five checkpoints for measurement systems:

Checkpoint 1. Make sure that all team members know and agree on the key objectives of the project in clear, measurable terms.

Checkpoint 2. Agree on milestones for each key objective; check for alignment with other internal goals and external issues.

Checkpoint 3. Assign individual and/or team accountability for objectives and milestones.

Checkpoint 4. Identify existing measures that will generate data to track progress; agree on baseline data.

Checkpoint 5. Identify any new measures that will need to be put in place to pick up critical data.

A detailed plan helps you monitor progress in a timely, accurate manner. Review each specific project metric that you have identified against this list of effective attributes and make any warranted adjustments.

Completeness. The extent to which a measure adequately measures the phenomenon instead of only some aspect of the phenomenon.

Timeliness. The extent to which a measurement can be taken soon after the need to measure.

Visibility. The extent to which a measure can be openly tracked by those being measured.

Controllability. The extent to which the measure can be directly influenced by those being measured.

Cost. Whether the measure is inexpensive, that is, making use of data easily obtained or already being collected for some other purpose.

Interpretability. The degree to which a measure is easy to understand and produces data that is readily comparable to other measures and/or time periods.

Importance. Whether the measure is connected to important business objectives, rather than being measured merely because it is easy to measure.

Change Process Profile

This tool repeats the test done at the beginning of the project (see Figure 3, page 3). At this point, the project should have made good progress, and you should have taken the needed steps in the areas of leading change, creating a need, shaping a vision, and mobilizing commitment. It is appropriate to reexamine the status of your overall change management actions now, particularly with respect to the three remaining areas of monitoring progress, finishing the job, and anchoring the change.

In a team meeting, have the core team assess the extent to which the activities in each category are established and effective.

Use the "Two out of Three" Rule:

- For successful initiation, two of the first three categories must be greater than 50 percent.

- To assure change is well rooted, two of the last three categories must be greater than 50 percent.

- *Mobilizing commitment* must always be greater than 50 percent.

Review your team's scoring and talk about your status. By now you will have significant experience in judging your organization's acceptance of the change effort you are completing. Make sure that you have sufficiently addressed the elements in the change model that come near the end: finishing the job and anchoring the change. A more detailed discussion of these two elements follows in the next chapters.

Force-Field Analysis

This tool provides a good method for assessing a project's likelihood of completion. It is effective in determining the forces aligned both for and against the project's success. It can be done in the middle of the project to serve as a check on progress. It can also be done at the beginning of a project to identify forces that need to be mitigated.

To begin, draw a T-shaped figure on a flip chart or whiteboard. Ask team members to name forces that are helping the project reach successful completion. List each force on the left with an arrow pointed to the right. Then, ask for forces *hindering* the project. List these forces on the right with arrows pointing left. (See Figure 10.)

Here are some potential forces, which could be either enablers or restraints, depending on your circumstances. Use these examples if the team starts slowly:

- Clear sponsorship and management commitment

- Sufficient funding

- Dedicated people (not overwhelmed by other priorities)

- Organizational understanding and support

- Practical schedule commitments

In concept, the force-field diagram is much like a football play: if the forces working in your favor overpower the forces that restrain you, you will move towards your goal. If not, you will either reach an impasse or actually lose ground.

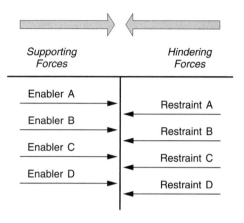

Figure 10   Force-field diagram.

Reinforcements	Supporting Forces	Hindering Forces	Mitigation Plans
Reinforcing factor 1 →	Enabler 1 →	← Restraint 1	Mitigator 1 →
Reinforcing factor 2 →	Enabler 2 →	← Restraint 2	Mitigator 2 →
Reinforcing factor 3 →	Enabler 3 →	← Restraint 3	Mitigator 3 →
Reinforcing factor 4 →	Enabler 4 →	← Restraint 4	Mitigator 4 →

Figure 11   Expanded force-field diagram.

Once the enabling and hindering forces are identified, you can systematically address them. For each enabling force, you can evaluate ways to strengthen it or assure its continuing effectiveness. For each restraining force, you can design methods to mitigate it.

Use an expanded diagram such as the one in Figure 11 to facilitate team discussion. *This helps ensure that the change becomes integrated into the fabric of the organization before the project runs out of steam.*

A force-field analysis was conducted at a sophisticated manufacturer of syringe products and magnetic resonance equipment. The team analyzed a technical issue concerning the best approach to a sterilization process. First, they established the major helping forces and hindering forces with respect to the proposed change in sterilization methods. Then they identified reinforcing factors for each helping force and mitigating factors for each hindering force. In this manner, they were able to consider all technical factors and take the appropriate actions to assure success of the project.

Force-Field on E-Beam Sterilization *All sterilization via ETO*			
Reinforcements	**Helping Forces/Pros**	**Hindering Forces/Cons**	**Mitigation Plans**
Sterilization capacity must be increased within the next 5 years ⟶	E-Beam offers increased throughput and capacity ⟵	Possibility of increased material costs	Perform material research and testing ⟶
Inventory interest charges are reduced ⟶	Reduction of post-sterile quarantine due to E-Beam results in significant benefits. ⟶	Possible need for tooling changes	Use radiation-stable plastics for all new products ⟶
E-Beam will reduce inventory space requirements ⟶			Work with molder to reduce/minimize cost ⟶
E-Beam provides a one-time cost avoidance in replacing inventory ⟶		Will require packaging or process change ⟵	Look to offset switching costs with cost reductions ⟶
E-Beam can facilitate private group labeling ⟶	E-Beam improves our flexibility and order taking ability ⟶	Need to submit 510K's on modified ⟵ products	
E-Beam can facilitate custom products ⟶		Possibility of product degradation over time ⟵	Perform real-time age testing on a broad range of materials ⟶
E-Beam can facilitate new product introduction ⟶		Large investment required ⟵	Contract portion of business via E-Beam first ⟶
E-Beam does not rely on gas penetration ⟶	E-Beam will provide savings through decreased inspection ⟶	Long implementation period ⟵	Keep option open by initiating testing now ⟶
	E-Beam will provide direct labor savings in sterilization ⟶	Significant resources, that is, project costs to implement ⟵	Reflect in financial model ⟶

Continued

Continued

Reinforcements	Helping Forces/Pros	Hindering Forces/Cons	Mitigation Plans
	E-Beam will provide direct material savings in sterilization ——▶	◀—— Disposition of ETO equipment unclear	Research options such as resale, contract ETO sterilization, and so on ——▶
Cardboard gage reduction possible due to no steam conditioning phase ——▶	E-Beam allows greater opportunity for package cost reduction ——▶	◀—— All current residual specifications are being met	
Potential substitution of paper for Tyvek due to no gas permeability required ——▶	E-Beam allows greater opportunity for package cost reduction ——▶	◀—— Cost of qualification/ validation greater than ETO	
	E-Beam equipment will occupy less space ——▶	◀—— Fear of job loss	
	E-Beam reduces risk with respect to European ETO residual restrictions ——▶	◀—— Currently operate state-of-the-art ETO processing facility	ETO process knowledge needs expanded throughout operation ——▶
	E-Beam will provide utility savings ——▶	◀—— Much easier to implement another ETO system, less capital, experienced personnel	
	ETO system will have some salvage value ——▶	◀—— Newest sterilizer is not fully depreciated	Gain experience base before making major investment and jeopardizing Medrad's #1 money maker ——▶
	No ETO residuals ——▶	◀—— Why take an unnecessary financial loss on ETO	ETO investments are a sunk cost ——▶
		◀—— B product only validated for ETO	Contract sterilize B product ——▶
			Validate B products for E-Beam ——▶

Step 6: Finishing the Job

Every change initiated will compete for time, resources, and attention. People often spend most of the available time on the launch of an initiative when it is new, rather than on trying to finish it after potentially months of work. But change efforts most often fail in the *execution* phases, rather than in the initial period.

WHY DO THIS?

The near-end of a project can be a delicate stage. The project work is complete, or nearly complete, but the new effort usually has not yet gone live. At this point, the majority of the people affected by the change have not had to face the new reality. People who have paid lip service to the change now have to live with it or else try to ignore it or even sabotage it. It is very important here to preserve the momentum of the project and announce clearly and with total management support, "Effective next Monday, all employees will use the new system."

At this point in the project, team members can feel burnt out and lack energy. Also, they have been so focused on doing the work that they may not appreciate that others have not been sufficiently prepared to change their behavior. This can be especially true in technical teams, since by their nature they focus on technical issues rather than behavioral ones.

For these reasons, it is particularly important to focus on *finishing the job*. The team should use the tools in this section to assure that the key elements are in place to complete the project and to assure that it gains acceptance within the organization.

During this step, there are several desired outcomes:

- A clear sense of the official start day for the new system.

- A clear understanding in the organization of the new system and sufficient commitment to implement it successfully.

- Consistent, visible, and tangible reinforcement of the change initiative in the organization.

- Integration of the new initiative with ongoing work activities.

If this step is not completed, there can be serious consequences:

- You will probably underestimate the time and effort required for the successful implementation of the change.

- Activities might be poorly coordinated.

- Competing activities may distract management and divert attention.

- The organization might not accept the change.

- Doubters and resisters may quietly refuse to make changes and make the project appear to fail.

TOOLS FOR FINISHING THE JOB

Sustained change occurs when change leaders and agents build and implement strategies for making change last. These tools provide practical methodologies to assure that the project is brought to completion:

1. *Reinforcement.* Use this tool to encourage positive behavior and results, and to associate your project with success in the public eye.

2. *Pilot run.* Use this tool to "shake out" any unforeseen problems with the implementation of the project, and to begin implementation on a smaller, less risky scale.

3. *Training.* Use training to educate your target audience about how to take advantage of the new process, system, and so on, that you are implementing.

Reinforcement

As each milestone of the change project is realized, the sponsor and team leader should arrange for public celebration and acknowledgment. This demonstrates to the organization that the project is supported. It also shows the team members that their efforts are recognized. Use these ideas to create effective and fun reinforcement:

- Create quick victories and celebrate them. Show what success looks like.

- Catch people doing things *right*. Give them immediate, sincere verbal recognition. This is probably the most effective form of recognition.

- Encourage team members to recognize each other during team meetings. Encourage members of one department to recognize members from another department. Also, if nonproject people help with an aspect of the team effort, reward them with recognition in front of the team, to their manager, in a newsletter, and so on. This is a very effective way to promote acceptance of the project.

- Create simple recognition events and rewards. Consider such things as pizza lunches, team T-shirts, Friday happy hour, and team coffee cups. Avoid extravagant and expensive rewards—these tend to focus people on the reward instead of the business goal. Focus on fun and cool ideas that help give the project an identity. This helps both internal team-building and external publicity.

- Tie in project successes with any existing reward and recognition systems.

The example on page 66 shows how positive team behavior regarding recognition influenced positive behavior on the executive level.

Pilot Runs

Most projects could benefit from a pilot run: the introduction of the change in a small, well-defined, and easily controlled area. This limits the consequences of any failures and allows a cycle of lessons learned to be incorporated into the final product. It also supports faster overall completion of a new process since it cuts down on false starts. Many companies have learned to *require* pilot runs of new products, having concluded that it saves overall time and effort.

At an FDA-regulated manufacturing plant, one team was working on how to review and process vendor-supplied instructions for using medical devices. The print quality was often deficient, and the actual instructions sometimes did not reflect the correct usage of the equipment. The team was trying to improve the reliability and quality of the printed material.

At the same time, unknown to the first team, a production manager was reviewing a sophisticated machine that allowed in-house printing of technical documents. He was motivated by cost and turnaround time.

Team members found out about this effort and arranged a demonstration. Since the team included the quality director, the production manager expressed some initial reservations, but he quickly saw the common interests of both efforts.

The machine's demonstration proved to be a success, producing in-house documents of high quality at a much lower cost and faster speed. Both the production manager and the team supported its purchase and use.

Subsequently, the team sent a letter to its executive sponsor, the vice president of marketing, telling him about a rare triple play of reengineering: lower cost, faster speed, and higher quality. As was appropriate, the team credited the production manager with reviewing and purchasing the new machine.

The sponsoring executive then recognized the production manager in an executive team meeting and used this situation as an example of the types of cross-functional synergy that the company was trying to promote. This was especially significant since the production function reported up through an entirely separate management structure, and it was much more common to promote *in-department* successes than other department's success.

To implement a pilot run, start with a very focused area in order to contain any problems that occur. For example, limit the scope to one day, one shift, one product line, or a similar approach. It helps to use a friendly part of the organization, such as a group that has a vested interest in the successful outcome of the project, although sometimes it is wise to involve some skeptics in the early stages of rollout.

As you discover any problems, incorporate revisions to your project and try the revised system in another area. Occasionally, it makes sense to implement a new system in stages, that is, implement in one location on March 1, in a second location on April 1, and so on. Use the successes that you have in the early stages to promote the system to later adoptors.

Be especially alert to encourage early-stage cheerleaders to share their endorsements with others in the organization. You will occasionally find that your biggest supporter is a manager from an early pilot run, who was involved in finding some bugs and fixing them. There is nothing like personal involvement to make a person feel a sense of ownership and responsibility.

If all other considerations are equal, try to pick an area for the pilot run that is representative of the organization as a whole. For example, you might pick a location that has most of the functions of the company as a whole but with a small group of people. You will want to test all of the "features" of your new system but in such a way as to limit the risk.

If a pilot run is not practical, consider a mock-up. That is, do all of the steps and actions called for but use dummy objects, forms, and so on. Physically walk through the entire process, step by step, as written in your procedure or instructions. Ask a neutral, uninitiated observer to work with you: implementing the process verbatim, playing devil's advocate, asking questions, and pointing out potential pitfalls.

In some cases, even a mock-up may not be practical. For example, you may be doing a proof of concept, or the prototype materials may not be available, or you may not have access to the location where the new system will be put into place.

In these cases, you can do a tabletop demo. This is a form of pilot run implemented almost exclusively by thought: the participants select roles and then talk their way through the process, step by step, filling out demo forms and trying various scenarios. Although this type of exercise cannot bring the same rigor to bear on the process you are testing, it still can uncover unanticipated problems with far less risk than no testing at all.

The examples on pages 68 and 69 show how a pilot run can be implemented successfully.

Training

In recent years, many companies have introduced sophisticated and complex information technology systems. All too often, these systems either fail or meet significant resistance for reasons that have nothing to do with their technical capabilities. They failed because the organization did not design a training program that made the intended users feel comfortable with the new process.

A high-tech manufacturing company lacked a way to receive returned goods into stock. Engineers would routinely tag the goods as *nonconforming* and segregate them in *the cage*—a holding location—while they started a laborious and time-consuming process of individually evaluating the items. Many goods had collected, and a new cage was built. Finally the goods spilled into the manufacturing floor, where it received management's attention.

A team of people was put together from the affected departments. They designed a logical process to bring undamaged items back into stock.

Since there was pressure to fix the space problems, most of the team wanted to issue the appropriate procedure and implement the solution immediately. The quality assurance representative, however, wanted to test the new process by holding a pilot run. After a brief debate, the team agreed to hold a quick pilot run.

An area foreman played the *pilot*, and moved the materials back into stock. It quickly became evident that staging of the materials would not work as designed. The returned materials disrupted the flow of the work on the line.

The team made some minor changes in how materials were staged and fixed the problems. The team went on to implement the new process and saved the company tens of thousands of dollars annually.

The change team no doubt had a clear idea of how useful the new system would be—they just failed to communicate this usefulness to the organization through good training. Lack of training can undercut even the most effective new system.

Training should comprise a significant subproject within the overall project. Consider obtaining the services of a professional trainer. Also, consider inviting nonproject personnel to participate in determining training needs. This provides a good opportunity to involve some key neutral people, and win their support.

To plan effective training, first consider what knowledge and skills the new program will require. Then consider the gap between that and the current skill level.

Since training has such a critical role, it should be tested during the pilot run. The best way to do this is to give an uninvolved person the prescribed training or instructions and ask them to go to work *without any*

A design and manufacturing facility was growing and needed a user-friendly system for developing its employees. They put a performance evaluation system in place, but were getting low response rates, particularly from some engineering and marketing groups.

A group of managers got together to understand why the current system was not working and to design a new system. They invited participation, particularly from the low-use groups.

They discovered several factors for the low usage of the current system. The system required feedback every month, which most people considered too frequent. The feedback for an employee came only from the boss, which people did not consider fair. Feedback results were used to influence salary increases. And the engineering and marketing employees thought that the current system was forced on them by the human resources department.

In light of the data, the managers designed a new system. They changed the frequency from monthly to twice per year. They used a 360° feedback system, so that each person got input from a wide range of employees. They removed the employee development process from the salary process. And they decided to design and test the new process with the engineers, and not implement it until the engineers were convinced that the new process would work. In fact, the team used engineers to implement an extensive pilot run.

At first, the engineers were skeptical and found many flaws in the details of the system. Each time, the team took actions to correct the flaws. The engineers became more interested in the process mechanics, in much the same manner that they might get involved in a new product launch. As the process got smoother, the engineers started defending the new process to other skeptics. By the end of the project, some engineering managers were advocating the new process in their staff meetings.

When the team introduced the new process, they already had the support of the most vocal critics of the older process. The rest of the organization followed suit. For these reasons, in large part, the new process was used by virtually 100 percent of the organization.

further coaching. If this test works, you can feel more confident that most people will understand.

Technically oriented project members often underestimate the amount of effort that training requires. For example, one hour of new training material, complete with handouts, can easily take eight or more hours to create. Also, the logistics of reserving rooms, scheduling busy people, coordinating production of materials, and so on, can make training a critical-path item. *Don't neglect this critical activity. Training comprises the delivery system for a major change effort.*

Step 7: Anchoring Change in Systems and Structures

This final step in the change management process assures that the change becomes embedded in and reinforced by the operational systems in place in the organization.

WHY DO THIS?

Successful changes can require a significant realignment of the organizational infrastructure. The change needs to be anchored in the culture and the environment, and reinforced by all systems such as the organizational structure, training and development, rewards and recognition, compensation, and promotion practices. The desired vision can only be fully realized if all of these systems are aligned and integrated with it.

During this step, there are two desired outcomes:

- Identify the key system and structure areas that must be addressed to assure the success of the project over the long term.

- Align the systems and structures with the desired behaviors.

If this step is not completed, there can be serious consequences:

- The new system could be undercut by the status quo.

- People might not internalize the change within the organization.

- The organization may need new competencies to fully implement the change and find that it lacks them. Unprepared employees could fail to endorse the new system, causing it to fail.

TOOLS FOR ANCHORING THE CHANGE IN SYSTEMS AND STRUCTURES

Long-lasting, effective change requires a thorough examination and realignment of key organization systems and structures. These tools provide practical methodologies to assure that the change is sufficiently internalized in the organization:

1. *Candidates for changed systems and structures.* Use this tool to determine which existing organizational systems and processes may need to be updated in order to integrate the change.

2. *Staffing and development needs.* Use this tool to evaluate whether you need to hire new people or develop skills of current employees in order to make full use of the change you are working on.

3. *Planning for integration.* Use this tool to determine the likely response of the organization, and to plan any corrective actions that may be warranted.

Candidates for Changed Systems and Structures

Have the team use the matrix in Table 7 to identify organizational systems that may need to be changed in order to support the change you have introduced. Brainstorm any other topics that you might need to add to the list. For each topic, assign a consensus rating based on the following:

- How critical is the topic for success? (*1* = not at all and *5* = extremely critical)

- How much work is needed to prepare? (*1* = not much and *5* = a lot)

Staffing and Development Needs

This exercise should be aimed at the desired behaviors identified in *shaping the vision*. It is best done in a team setting and preferably with a human resources professional present.

Table 7 Candidates for changed systems and structures.

Topic	Critical for the Project? (1–5)	Amount of Work Needed? (1–5)	Remarks
Staffing: New talent that we have to recruit and place to support the initiative.			
Development: Training and preparation of the employees.			
Measures: How we track ongoing performance.			
Rewards: How we recognize/reward desired behavior.			
Communication: How we use information to build and sustain momentum.			
Organizational design: How we are organized to support the change initiative.			

Consider all of the competencies needed within the organization—technical, cultural-political, interpersonal—and from external sources to make the new system work over the long term. Ask the team to brainstorm a list of these competencies and record them in the first column of a table. (See Table 8). Then, prioritize them according to importance.

Then complete the remaining columns for each competency. Consider whether the competencies exist now, whether they need to be developed, or whether they need to be brought in by recruiting or outsourcing.

Lastly, take an honest look at how well your organization has developed needed human capabilities in the past. If you have any concerns, take them to your sponsor and to your human resources department.

Don't neglect this aspect, even if it does seem out of scope to some team members. Remember, if the project fails over the long term because of lack of needed training and development, it will reflect badly on all members of the team, no matter how out of scope it seemed.

Table 8   Staffing and development needs.

What knowledge, skill, personal characteristics are required?	To what extent do they exist?	How will we obtain or develop the talent we need?	How effective have we been at developing talent in the past?

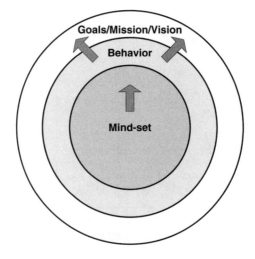

Figure 12   Mind-set and behavior.

Planning for Integration

This tool lets your team assess how well your business environment will promote the acceptance of the change you are making. Acceptance is defined here as *engaging in the desired behavior.* Behavior is influenced by internal values and principles, or *mind-set,* which has been addressed previously and which is illustrated in Figure 12. Behavior is also influenced by external factors such as an organization's reward and recognition practices and by its metrics.

Consider the desired behavioral change you want from members of the organization; for example, *people will use the computerized system to track change orders and not require paper copies.* Then use the following list to consider how your reward system and business metrics will either promote or discourage this behavior. Take action where needed, both to assure positive consequences and to remove inadvertent negative consequences:

- If an employee carries out each of the desired behaviors, what is likely to be the organization's response—reward/approval, punishment/disapproval, no reaction, or impossible to predict?

- How will the desired behavior receive positive recognition?

- What are existing rewards—financial and nonfinancial?

- How could we reward the desired behaviors that are not now being rewarded?

- What are the existing metrics in this area?

- Which existing measures might provide information about any of the desired behaviors?

- How could we measure those desired behaviors that are not now being measured?

- If we achieve the desired changes, which existing measure will emit false signals, erroneously indicating that performance is degrading?

In the end, you will have done everything possible to promote acceptance of the change, having addressed both the internal factors, such as motivation and commitment, and the external factors, such as rewards, recognition, and metrics.

Conclusion

Changes within organizations have two components: the technical and the human. Both have to work. Too often, sponsors and teams focus only on the technical aspects, rather than the messy, people-centered aspects. But, in fact, few changes fail because of technical inadequacy—after all, they were designed by professionals and approved by the organization.

When change fails, it is usually because of the human aspects—that is, the failure or reluctance of the affected people to embrace the change. In the author's experience, these types of failures far exceed those failures caused by technical inadequacies such as misengineered features.

Before you initiate a change, make sure that your organization can handle it. Organizations can absorb only so much change; if you ask too much of an organization, it might founder.

If you decide to charter a change effort, make sure that you have obtained the support required: sponsorship, people, money, and so on. Use the tools herein to measure the levels of support and your likelihood for success. They are designed to be easily applied and to break down the messy business of human acceptance of change into more or less quantitative elements that should especially appeal to technical professionals.

Pay attention to the actions required to *make change work*. Your project depends on it. Best wishes!

Bibliography and Resources

Burack, Elmer, and Florence Torda. *The Manager's Guide to Change.* New York: Brace-Park Press, 1989.

Connor, Daryl. *Managing at the Speed of Change.* New York: Random House, 1993

Kotter, John. *Leading Change.* Boston: Harvard Business School Press, 1996.

Pendlebury, John, et al. *Ten Keys to Successful Change Management.* New York: John Wiley and Sons, 1998.

Pritchett, Price. *Business As UnUsual.* Plano, TX: Pritchett & Associates, 1994.

———. *High-Velocity Culture Change.* Plano, TX: Pritchett & Associates, 1993.

———. *Resistance: Moving beyond the Barriers to Change.* Plano, TX: Pritchett & Associates, 1996.

Prosci. *Best Practices in Managing Change.* Loveland, CO: Prosci Research, 2000.

Reader Feedback

I am interested in keeping this knowledge and these tools current. I would like to hear about your examples, lessons learned, horror stories, new tools to use, and so on. If your examples are included in future editions of this work, I will include full attribution to you and your organization, as desired. Please write to me at:

ASQ Quality Press
Attention: Brien Palmer
600 N. Plankinton Ave.
Milwaukee, WI 53203
USA

Index